The Minimalist Millennial

Declutter Your Space, Reduce Your
Stress, and Live a Balanced Life

By: Brit McGinnis

www.britmcginnis.com

Published by 𝆕 Archangel Ink

ISBN: 1942761260
ISBN-13: 978-1-942761-26-6

Table of Contents

Introduction

I became a minimalist when I was 23 years old.
This is also when I realized that books about minimalism suck.

Seriously, I hate books about minimalism. They are no freaking fun. Ninety percent of the time, they're written by older people who have already "made it" and can now live as minimalists on the backs of their established success. Seriously, forty-year-old dudes loooove to talk about how minimalist they are. It's really funny.

As a result, their claim that anyone can be a minimalist is often answered with a resounding "Puh-shaw! Yeah, right! Of course you can reduce hours and work on de-stressing your life; you've already made it!"

Those detractors are absolutely right. The people who have already made their money usually have a much easier time becoming minimalist.

Older people, or just those who found success early in life, can afford to reduce their hours at work for the sake of stress. They can "downgrade" to having no car and not suffer the consequences. These people can stop buying name-brand groceries and instead eat food from overpriced farmer's markets (you know, to minimize their carbon footprint). They can downsize to only a few name-brand dress shirts and live. Oh, the sacrifice!

These people make minimalism look bad.

And yet, they're not as bad as the minimalism extremists. These people are often at the other end of the spectrum age-wise, typically young college students. They hear about minimalism and wig out as if they've found the meaning of life. They drop everything and head off the grid, condemning any physical property a person could ever want. "Is that a new water bottle? Ha! You poor saps, I remember back when I was a slave to consumerism too."

These people also make minimalism look bad. They're also jerks, but that's beside the point.

I'm here to tell you, as a low- to middle-income twentysomething, that anyone can be a minimalist. You don't need a sackful of money to do it, but you also don't need to go full zero on owning stuff.

Minimalism is about living a life of balance. More often than not, this involves owning less stuff.

It's a hard thing, owning less stuff. It's hard to get rid of certain types of stuff. But it's absolutely worth it. The balance you find from reducing your stuff is absolutely worth it. Trust me on that.

But more than just reducing stuff, minimalism is also a balance-seeking way of life. It's a no-bullshit, heart-driven, brutally analytical way of living life. It's also really freaking fun.

Thank you for picking up this book. I'm excited to "talk" with you about minimalism here, and I say that because I don't intend to lecture you. If you want a lecture on minimalism, there are lots of other books and webinars where you can find that.

I'm here to share my story of becoming a minimalist, and talk about what it means to become a minimalist as a member of the Millennial generation. It DOES mean something different for us, because the whole idea of living with less stuff doesn't feel like as much of a choice as it used to. We've become used to downsizing as a way of life—in terms of stuff and expectations alike.

So I'm proposing a new kind of minimalism. A kind based on focus, and looking at what you want for your *entire* life. We're all downsizing on stuff. But to what end? And how do we get rid of our stuff and genuinely not miss it?

Be warned: I will curse, rant, and gush about minimalism. It genuinely changed my life, so I definitely gush about it from time to time. I promise, I'll keep it to the bare minimum. Be all minimalist about it…

Just like everything in life, probably not all of this will apply to you. That's fine! Take what you like from this book and leave the rest. All I want to do is talk about minimalism in a different way. In a more *approachable* and *realistic* way.

Hopefully this will get you thinking about how much stuff you really need to be happy. I guarantee, it's less than you think. But again, take what you want from here and leave whatever doesn't make sense.

Just sayin', it'd be cool to run into one of you at a garage sale at some point.

1

We Are Taught To Love Stuff

You know what the biggest reason to become a minimalist is? Yearbooks.

Someone please tell me why we still have yearbooks. They're giant books of photographs of people you barely care about anymore. Full of phone numbers that don't work. Photographic evidence that you indeed went through an awkward phase.

Seriously, have we not yet evolved to the point where photographers can send parents digital copies of their kids' photos? There have been incidents now where principals have airbrushed girls to be more "modest" in their photographs. You're seriously telling me we can't send parents digital copies of school photos?

Also, Facebook exists. It exists in full. Kids no longer need to solicit friends for well wishes and ask pretty people for their phone numbers.

So why do yearbooks still exist? They're big, they're clunky, and they're pretty much useless at this point in history.

Yearbooks exist because schools need to make money, and yearbooks are a great way to do it.

Legacy is the only thing really driving the appeal of yearbooks at this time. There's really very little else marking their appeal. For a long time, they were the default way to commemorate a school year. Now that they've been officially outmoded, they've become a nostalgia buy. Parents remember yearbooks, so they buy them for their kids, who then go on to never read them.

We buy yearbooks for the same reason we buy a lot of things: We're taught to buy it. We're told that we "need" it to be socially competent.

Nine out of ten times, you don't need whatever that thing is.

Do you really *need* to buy that new fashionable item that's coming into fashion this season? If it's a flash in the pan, it'll pass and you'll be out a hundred bucks. Do you *need* that new smartphone? Unless you think you'll use most of the new features, better just hang on to your current setup. You'll be thankful once your next bill comes.

In an economy where most people have their basic needs met, companies have to get creative with how they extract money from us. They have to be really devious about how they try to get rich. This strategy mostly consists of them *making needs up*.

How do I know this? Because, dear people, I used to work in the start-up world.

Ah, the nonsense that powers the start-up world. It runs on wish dust and fairy magic, all in the hands of start-up founders. They spend hours upon hours trying to figure out how to make the next big thing people will want to do with their phones. And if they can't figure something out, they will make something up.

I was proud of the work I did in the start-up world. I do many similar things today as a virtual assistant. But I was very lucky in that I landed a job in a company (which is now defunct) that provided an extremely tangible service to its customers. They came up with and tried to sell a service that people could genuinely use. Good for them.

The other 90 percent of startups I ran into during my time were always looking for The Next Cool App That People Didn't Even Know They Wanted. Not trying to solve existing problems, but inventing hot new things that people would then buy out for millions of dollars. They weren't listening to what their customers said they wanted. They were building things and then convincing people that they wanted them.

I thought that was crazy. But once I left the tech world, I realized that these sales tactics were everywhere. People are being screamed at from all sides to buy electronics, subscription services, exclusive fashions, steep leases, and swag from their favorite TV shows. We don't need any of it to survive, and yet we're practically being told that we do.

Try this, just to see what I'm talking about: Don't buy anything for an entire week. Absolutely nothing. Just pay bills and get whatever you need to survive that week.

Now look at your Facebook feed and see what people talk about having bought that week. It'll stun you.

And look, I'm not saying that buying stuff isn't fun. I love the feeling of buying stuff. It makes me feel like an adult. I'm taking care of business. I've made it far enough along that I can buy stuff with my own money. It feels great!

But buying stuff should feel joyful, and it shouldn't be coerced. If I spend time contemplating a purchase for a while and *then* buy it, it feels a million times more rewarding than rushing out and getting something trendy that I'll probably have to return at the end of the season. When your head AND heart are involved, you'll be much more likely to walk away with something you really care about.

Also, standing in line for a new smartphone with five hundred other people is never as fun as it looks. Ditto with books and movies. Woohoo, we all got the same thing! All right!

I know, I know, people come for the *community experience* of it all. But is it really a community experience when the point is to be sold stuff by a company? There's only so many times you can say,

"I'm so excited for this" and "What are you looking forward to most in the next book?" before you start to feel like you're being shuffled toward a consumerism worship event.

Again, I'm *not* saying buying things is bad. I'm saying that it shouldn't be done under duress. Millennials have less money than previous generations, something that hasn't been seen in a long time. It's a unique situation!

Companies don't really know what to do with us. How should they market their goods to one of the poorest generations in decades? So they're just pushing shiny things out as usual and seeing what happens. And the sad thing is, we keep buying them. We have no money, yet we spend like we have all the money in the world.

You don't have to buy nothing ever to be a minimalist. That's stupid and unrealistic. But the first step is to look around and try to understand all the messages telling you to buy things you don't need. You need much less to survive (or even just to be happy!) than you think. In the next chapter, we'll talk about identifying those core things that you personally need.

But before you go on to the next chapter, I highly recommend not buying anything for one week. Just as an experiment. The voices and messages telling you to BUY ALL THE THINGS will feel louder than ever.

And coincidentally, they'll be easier to ignore.

2

Identify Your Basic Tools

No matter what anyone tells you, you don't need to get rid of 100 percent of your stuff to become a minimalist.

Seriously, ignore those people. They're living in a fantasy.

This is the 21st century. You need a certain amount of stuff to live and be successful. Even to go fully off the grid, you still need tools and shit. Probably more technology than the average person, just to make sure you're scrambling every signal from The Man effectively.

The key to successful minimalism is determining that bare minimum amount of stuff that you need to survive, be sane, and be happy.

I'm including "be happy" because happiness is important. It is. I'm not saying that because I'm a hippie, I'm saying it because if you're not happy doing a certain lifestyle change, you'll stop doing it. We're simple creatures, us humans. If we don't like doing something and there's no great grand payoff, we'll eventually stop doing it. We want to be happy.

But this inherently means that everyone's list of Basic Tools for Life will be different. You may not have a bathroom scale as one of your Basic Tools. But it might be on the list for someone who tries to stay at a certain weight for their health.

Here's how I narrow down my list of Basic Tools:

- What do I use on a daily basis?
- What do I use on a weekly basis?
- What do I need for success in my work life?
- What makes me relax more than anything?

If my house caught on fire and burned down, what would I secretly be glad was gone? (DIE, school yearbooks!)

Notice how there are no definitive answers anywhere on this list. That's on purpose. Because you don't need a set number of Basic Tools. You need the bare minimum of what fits these qualifications, which is going to be different for everyone.

Let me give a *scandalous* example: I own a smartphone. This is friggin' rare in the minimalism community. There are many blogs decrying smartphones, talking about how they represent consumerist excess and are rotting all of our brains.

But here's the thing: I use my smartphone for work all the time. When I'm sent to live-tweet an event for promotion, I have my smartphone on and ready. I take photos for corporate accounts on Instagram. I answer e-mails from apps regularly, because I don't always have a desk for this kind of work. My smartphone is a Basic Tool for my life. Ditto with my laptop.

Now, this doesn't mean I stand in line every time a new smartphone or laptop is available. I haven't upgraded either Basic Tool in years. But I do need them, so I will not downgrade to a flip phone just because it is currently in vogue for minimalists. #youdontknowmylife

Compare this to my friend Miranda, whose Basic Tools include makeup reflecting the latest trends. She's much more likely to indulge in magenta lipstick or blue eye shadow than I am, and nicer brands too. But Miranda works in *fashion*. In *New York City*. I don't hold her to my standards of minimalism, because why would I? Her needs and circumstances as a New York fashionista are light years away from my needs and circumstances as a Pacific Northwest writer. It would be arrogant and dumb to hold everyone to my standards.

Honing this list down to the essentials takes as long as it takes. You'll probably find yourself doing it over and over. That's a good thing! I'm always cutting stuff out of my routine and trips to Goodwill are a regular occurrence in my house.

Again, like the constant pressure to buy stuff, what matters is your awareness about what you own. This isn't a book to teach you about how to organize your life into tubs and bookshelves. This a book meant to make you *think* differently.

Every time you consider making a purchase, think about whether it would qualify as one of your Basic Tools. Does reading make you relax more than anything? If so, then you can probably justify buying those books. You'll probably want to thin out your collection once you stop reading those books consistently, but that'll happen later.

Becoming a minimalist stuff-wise is a process. You don't have to run out and ditch everything to become an "official" minimalist. That's not how it works.

Again, this is why books on minimalism tend to suck. They preach minimalism at the cost of sanity. Instead of focusing on the mindset behind someone choosing to go minimalist, they're more interested in the sheer amount of stuff.

Meanwhile, I'm over here going, "Hey! Who wants to watch a movie on my Amazon Prime account?"

"WHAT?" the minimalists cry. "You own a ROKU? You're owned by stuff, man!"

"Um, no. I bought Amazon Prime so I wouldn't have as much physical crap lying around. And it makes my life a lot easier because I spend less time worrying about how much it costs to ship things."

"Uh…oh. Fine."

The main lesson here: Having stuff isn't always the problem. Having too much of the *wrong* stuff always is.

I've seen lots of examples of people going too minimalist for their own good. Take my friend Julia. She's an avid gamer, and is usually the first person I know to get a new console on the day it comes out. It makes her happy and connects her to friends. Party on.

But here's what inevitably happens whenever a new console comes out: Julia gathers up all of her old games and consoles and trades them in for credit, which she then uses to alleviate some of the cost of the new consoles (and usually a few games).

This *sounds* like a good idea, and like the good minimalist thing to do. But what happens when Julia starts feeling nostalgic about a game she used to play on an old system? She then has to buy a converted version made for the new console. She could hypothetically borrow one from a friend, but that's becoming a less viable option what with various companies no longer allowing transfers. Game rental companies are becoming more and more scarce, forcing many players to spend extra money just to have new versions of games they once owned.

Also, trading in old games for new games is a famously skewed practice. You may have spent $50 on that game last year, but you may only get $15 for it when you bring it back to the store to trade it in for cash or credit. It may even be the same store you originally purchased the game at. Tough noogies.

If Julia had kept every console she had ever traded in, she probably would have saved herself hundreds of dollars over the years. She would also have those consoles to replay outdated games, lend to other people just trying them out, or even rent them to others through an online service. There's also a major issue with video game preservation. If Julia had held on to her old consoles and donated them to one of the rapidly multiplying video game museums, she'd probably be just as happy seeing them preserved as she would have been saving five dollars on the latest console. In fact, knowing how much of a gamer Julia is, she'd probably be even happier.

Becoming a minimalist stuff-wise is easier than anyone thinks. You don't have to get rid of everything under the sun. You just have to learn to *question* everything that you buy and own. Far fewer purchases are as necessary as they seem. And far more purchases bog you down than you may think.

3

Money Follows You

I could write an entire chapter on debt and how it relates to minimalism. In fact, I almost did. But that would have been obnoxious of me.

Besides, I'm still working through my student debt. I didn't want to be a complete hypocrite about "blasting through your student debt!" (Now imagine that as a sensationalist blog post title!)

But I wanted to share something that I learned about debt, money, patience, and not fucking around.

The first two years I was out of college, I completely floundered. I took jobs at startups, stand-alone companies, and even one at a health food company. I was swimming without direction, just trying to get my head above water and *start paying off my student loans.*

Oh gosh, those loans. Over $20,000 of stressful nonsense.

My parents couldn't help support me through college, and back then, we thought taking out loans was the norm. So I took them out again and again, just trying to survive.

Post-college, the internship that I thought would surely hire me didn't. So I put my writing career on hold to look for "real work." After realizing that "real work" sucked, I re-invested my time into writing and have since had a great career. It's fledgling, but it's coming along. Hooray!

But my student loans are still there.

Haunting me.

Pressuring me to give up my career.

Telling me to get a conventional job so I can earn more money.

Then I can make payments on them, and maybe they'll go away after…

Insidious.

But those are loans for you. That's their nature. When you take out a loan or sign up for a credit card, that imaginary money follows you. You're chained to it.

One could argue that this is all part of growing up, and that all of the great milestones of adulthood require you to spend a lot of money, preferably money you don't have that you can repay in chunks later. It's just part of the American experience, so we should just deal with it.

To that I say, what are you smoking?

Are you telling me that in order to be a well-adjusted adult in a first-world country, you are required to go into thousands of dollars of debt? I have to have three credit cards, take out a car loan, sign a mortgage, take out private loans to pay for my wedding, and then refinance the house when times are tough or to pay for my child's college tuition?

In addition, I'm *also* required to save for retirement and medical emergencies? Plus upgrade my car every few years? Plus buy an iPod and laptop and...OH GOD, THE ROPE AROUND MY NECK IS TOO TIGHT!

Okay, it's off now.

Money *is* a rope. I mean that seriously. It can pull you out of a pit, or it can choke you to death.

The question for minimalists is, how do we use money in the way that will stress us out the least?

How can you use whatever money you have so that your life will be happiest for longer? So that you have the space and the mental energy to do what you want to do most?

I think you know what I'm getting at here.

Debt is not normal. So let's get rid of it.

I don't mean defer it so we can deal with it later. I mean, *let's get rid of it*. You, me, and everyone else we know. Let's stop pretending that we're not terrified of the incredible amount of money we owe to others and just go for it. Just take a few years and just pay off that son of a bitch.

Because even though we're trying to avoid the impact of student loans, it's still happening. It's holding us back from moving out, developing our careers, and feeling free to do whatever we truly want to do. You or someone you know will likely stay in a shitty job forever just because it helps pay off those student loan bills.

So why not just take a few years, work as much as you can, and just get those suckers out of the way?

I know this sounds insane. I know this sounds drastic and way too simple of an answer.

But I have to ask: Is paying a thousand dollars a month any less freeing than paying hundreds? Especially if it means you're done with that debt sooner?

Would you rather mainly spend on loans and not "fun stuff" for a little while but then be free to spend on "fun stuff" forever after that?

Aren't a few years of Hell better than a lifetime of Purgatory?

Okay, that was a little dramatic.

But I'm serious about this. I'm in the middle of an anti-debt journey of my own now, and I can tell you that nothing feels better than getting one up on my student loans. Nothing feels better than paying a bill a month early, then getting a little bit more in on the inside. It's fabulous.

Sure, I've made cutbacks. I didn't go to Comic Con with my friends because I spent more money than I originally planned to spend with them on the previous weekend. I haven't bought new clothes in months, and probably won't for another year. The majority of my money goes toward loans, not things that actively make me happy.

Most painfully, I had to drop my membership to my city's Junior League. For the uninitiated, Junior League is an organization with chapters in most major cities. It's part sorority, part National Honor Society.

But at its heart, Junior League is a band of merry women who do volunteer work in their cities and advocate on behalf of major charities in their area. They're also notorious for holding big charity events. It's awesome. But I couldn't justify spending hundreds of dollars a year in membership fees, plus invest time volunteering that could be spent working at jobs that would earn me money to pay off my debt. I couldn't justify it to myself, so I had to drop my membership pitch. It felt awful. I really wanted to be a part of that organization.

And yet…every time I pay into that loan, less money is following me. Fewer and fewer numbers drag me down. I feel free to live the life I want, because I have fewer pressures telling me to pay out.

To be a little evangelical about it, I want everyone I know to feel as happy as I do when I shrink my loan down. I want everyone to feel that free.

It makes sense that people don't just put their noses to the grindstone and just hammer out all their debt. It makes a *lot* of sense. Your twenties and thirties are supposed to be the time of your life when you make big strides in your career, not pay for the costly sin of going to college. I say that sarcastically, because it's not a friggin' sin to want some higher education.

It makes sense to want to spend your time and money on yourself, your career, and relationships. That stuff's important! The most successful person I know is a New York friend I'll call Miranda. She has a buttload of student loans. But she's deferred them year after year, instead investing her time and money covering Fashion Week for the online magazine she works for, where she's now a Very Important Editor, FYI.

Do I fault her? Not at all. She's doing what she thinks is absolutely necessary for her career.

Could I ever do what she's doing? Hell, no, I'd go insane.

I'll give Miranda this, though: She doesn't own a car. She doesn't own a house. She is a thrift store and discount shopping genius. She's reducing her debt in other ways, which I applaud.

What I'm trying to get at here is that it is 100 percent in your best interest to eliminate debt early on in your life. You really don't want to carry that around for the rest of your life.

I know it doesn't seem like a big deal now. It's just a few hundred dollars a month. You're probably making a lot more than that if you've managed to get a good job post-university. If you're in your early thirties, it probably feels like even less than that. It's just another bill.

But it's one of the few bills in life where you can control the amount you pay. This isn't just some bill you can pay and forget. You have the power to make it stop.

So why aren't you?

I ask because I know the answer: Because it would sabotage the quality of life you're used to now. Because it's uncomfortable. Because it feels like an impossibly high amount.

I get that. I totally do.

But living in denial of debt is *not fucking fun*. Knowing that you'll have to spend at least a good chunk of your life paying off a huge chunk of debt taints your perspective. It shadows so many of your decisions, in ways you may not even realize.

I know a couple, Tom and Amanda. They live in one of the towns I lived in for many years (my life has involved a lot of moving around!).

Both Amanda and Tom are both ambitious, but they have over a hundred thousand dollars in combined debt. Blame expensive schools. They're making payments faithfully, but there's a sense of urgency that's palatable whenever you visit their house.

It's an urgency that only exists in houses that have debt hanging over their heads. An urgency to live *now*, and live with extravagance because we'll be paying off this thing for the rest of our lives. It's why, even though they have the most debt out of anyone I know, they're also the ones with the most recent gaming consoles. And if my mom's to be believed, they're the first people from my circle of friends to have a kid.

I'm not against gaming consoles. I'm not against children. What I *am* against is making big purchases and/or life decisions in a major state of stress. If you feel like you're going to be paying off major debt for the rest of your life, that's a really crappy mindset to be making life decisions in. You're either living for today in fear of bills coming tomorrow or completely ignoring the bill, thus making it even more crippling once it does come.

So I'm inviting you to do something with me.

You ready?

Give yourself one year, and pay off half of your loans.

Not all of them, just half. This is what I'm doing this year, and I'm inviting you to join me in doing it.

Give yourself a minimum amount of money, and don't let your bank account grow above that. Put everything else into whatever loan you're currently paying off. If you make $800 every two weeks and you typically need $200 to pay off bills, make your minimum bank amount $300 (emergencies and forgotten birthdays happen, so we must have a cushion). Then dump the remaining $500 into whatever loan you're paying off with the most interest at the time.

If this doesn't work for you, try something else! But this year, let's eliminate half of our debt. Just half.

Make some sacrifices, have a few lean months. But let's eliminate half our debt together.

I say "together" because I'm totally doing this. My personal minimum is $200, so anything above that goes straight to my student loans. My credit card debt isn't killer, thank goodness. So I'm prioritizing my student loans this year.

It'll suck. It'll really blow. You will feel left out of things because you'll have to say no to paying for them.

But making those early payments will start feeling addictive. And I promise you it will take *years* of stress off your back by just doing one year of extreme payoff. Those are years you'll be able to spend working on your career, without having to worry about paying off your debt. You can be freer earlier than anyone ever plans for you to be! *You can stick it to the man.*

Let's do it. I'm tweeting about it at @BritMcGinnis, so feel free to bitch to me about how broke you feel. But I promise you—it'll be worth it! You'll feel so free afterward, you won't even know how to handle it.

4

Listen To What You REALLY Want

One New Year's Eve, I was pacing the floor of my office, drawing up the enthusiasm to go out and drink with friends.

I had been invited out by my friend Deena, but now I was 100 percent not feeling it. It'd be an hour to drive out and an hour to drive back home. Traffic would inevitably be terrible, and there was no guarantee that the good restaurants would have any good tables left.

I had already said yes. But it was like a PHYSICAL force was keeping me from going out. I was *really* not feeling it.

So my newly minimalist self called up my friend and told her I was going to pass after all. I stayed home and was watching *Scarface* when the clock struck midnight. It was perfect.

As we go through life, we learn what we want in our heart of hearts. It's not a matter of self-determination. It's a matter of sifting through the layers of expectation, pride, and the desire to look socially acceptable to the nuggets of truth underneath.

This is the part of the book where we're going to go into the "mindset" stuff. Basically, minimalism for your heart and brain. It won't be too touchy-feeling, I promise.

When it comes down to it, being an emotional minimalist means giving less and less of a shit about what other people think.

It's listening to your real desires and goals in their purest form, and following through on them. It's not being selfish, necessarily. Just embracing yourself and your needs exactly as they are.

This will come off as selfish to a lot of folks reading this right now. But I promise you, it isn't. It's treating every single one of your personal desires as valid.

If I want to watch a film one night and my boyfriend wants to play video games instead, I'll just give a him a kiss and go upstairs to watch a movie by myself. I'm honoring my own desire, because it's 100 percent just as valid as his. Even if I choose to play video games with him instead, I take a moment to consciously think, "I am *choosing* to play video games because right now, my desire for bonding time with my boyfriend is more important to me than doing *exactly* what I want on my own time."

This sounds cheesy, but it really does change your perspective on situations like that. You're rarely, if ever, the victim in awkward social situations.

Everything is a conscious choice, which not only feels amazing but ultimately leads to people respecting you.

All you have to do is sift through all the societal bullshit that can cloud your intuition.

For the longest time, my old friend Karina was in the worst kind of on-again-off-again relationship. She didn't know what she wanted, mainly because she was "trying to be a decent person" to the other person. She was also trying to "go with the flow" and "have an open mind."

I listened to this bullshit for exactly ten minutes and replied, "You sound miserable. Get out."

But she protested. And made excuses. And eventually left them to be with a much nicer person. She now counts that on-again-off-again relationship as a fling. I call it a prime example of not listening to your own intuition.

You know what you really want for yourself, deep down. You *know*. You know deep in yourself that you really want a burrito for dinner, not that salad you told yourself you were going to eat. Just admit it.

Have you admitted it?

Okay, good. Now make a case for yourself on why you should eat that salad. If you can. If you can't, just eat the freaking burrito.

You see how much simpler this is, rather than lying to yourself and eating everything in the fridge later on? It's really a much nicer way to live.

Not to say that emotional minimalists don't make goals or have zero discipline. On the contrary, living with less stuff and less emotional filter bullshit often opens the door for incredible discipline to come through. It's just that emotional minimalists don't bullshit themselves about what they actually want.

If I'm living with no bullshit, I'll freely admit that I still harbor a fantasy of being an author in New York City. Maybe that dream will come to pass, maybe it won't. But I still harbor it, even while I'm living and honing my craft in the Pacific Northwest.

And even as I think about that dream, I think about every financial decision that leads me away from it. I allow myself to look at my decision to buy a car—I could have saved that for a move to New York. How about excessive student loan payments? Those could have been saved up.

This process can be disheartening, but it's also incredibly liberating. It shows a person the extent of their own agency. If you don't like something, you have far more power to change it than you think.

It also opens up the biggest question of emotional minimalism: **If you're conflicted about whether you really want something, or haven't done anything to work toward a goal, you probably don't really want it that much.**

Go ahead, send me your hate thoughts. I dare you. Tweet at me. I'm at @BritMcGinnis. Tell me how outraged you are.

I'm betting that before you complete that tweet, you'll realize I'm right.

Not wanting something big or ambitious in life doesn't make you lazy. It just means you don't want it right now. And it means you'll be much happier acknowledging that you don't want it.

I don't want to live in New York right now, because I'd rather be financially secure at this point in my life. Eventually, sure! I'd love to move to New York when I'm financially secure. But I'd rather do it then than now, in the middle of my quest to pay off half my student debt. Plus, I'd like my boyfriend to be able to go and further his ambitions as well.

Oh, yes. I went there. I said I didn't want to do something because I want my *boyfriend* to be able to go along with me. #sotieddown

Nowhere is it more important to know what you want at any given time than when you're in a romantic relationship. If you're muddied and unclear in any other part of your life except that one, you can survive. But when it comes to the person you're dating/having sex with/are committed to for an indefinite amount of time, you *have* to be in touch with your own intuition. You *have* to be.

If you aren't, that's when things get really scary. That's when you start doubting everything about yourself. That's when you start disappearing into the other person. That's when you're afraid to say you want to be alone because you're afraid it will hurt their feelings. What kind of bullshit is that?

If you're not with someone who appreciates exactly what you want and may even help you get it, then you're in the wrong relationship. Ditto if you feel you need to stifle your desires to keep that person in your life.

You have to know what you want, and you have to have the ability to listen to yourself. It's too important.

I'm lucky enough to be with someone who supports my dream to live in New York as a writer. If I got a job at *The New Yorker* tomorrow, he'd buy my plane ticket and start applying to grad schools in the area so he could follow me.

But we had to *earn* that. I had to learn to listen to my own intuition, and learn to stick up for what I personally wanted even if it differed from what he wanted. We had to learn how to be different but happy, and how to treat each other's desires with equal respect.

Life is so much easier when you're in touch with your personal desires. If you learn how to stop worrying so much about what other people think and spend time learning to listen to your own fine self, everything will change.

You'll be able to go out or stay in knowing you made the choice to do so.

You'll know your own self better.

You'll be able to define goals better than ever.

You'll see the paths that your decisions led you down, and forgive yourself if it's not what you originally set out to do.

Sound appealing?

All you have to do to get there is *listen*. Just stand in one place, wherever you are. Or sit, if you're reading this on a train or something.

Just be still for a minute, and ask yourself what you want right now.

What do you want *now*?

Don't judge yourself for whatever you say. You can want to go home and go back to sleep. You can want a new smartphone to read this book on more easily. You can want to go home and make pancakes for your roommates because it didn't feel right leaving for work after that argument.

You can feel happy. You can feel tired. You can feel angry at having to go to your job, even though you have to pay the bills this month. *You are allowed those emotions.*

You don't have to deal with those emotions if you don't want to. Maybe you'll feel powerless, because you still have to go to work no matter how you may feel about it.

That's okay. Your emotions now "know" that you're aware of them. You'll most likely find yourself paying attention to them more and more.

You'll be inching a little but further toward a life of emotional minimalism, a.k.a. treating your emotions with the respect they deserve and eliminating unnecessary bullshit. Ain't it grand?

5

Define Adulthood for Yourself

Here's where I reveal a dirty little secret about myself: I'm one of those "lazy," "adulthood-delaying" Millennials who live at home with their parents.

It became necessary after college, because neither my boyfriend nor I had managed to find employment. The internship I was kicking butt at didn't hire me, and my boyfriend's industry shifted so that you needed a degree to get any gig worth a damn. So we were forced to camp out at home rather than go completely broke.

We've been here for a few years now, and have only managed to secure full-time employment in the last year. Things came and went, but we've only both found stuff with staying power in the last year. We're now working like dogs to save up and move out.

And you know what? I'm glad we did this. Yeah, most of our friends live in apartments with dogs and television sets. But chances are, their parents are paying for at least a third of their rent. They also may not own their own car, whereas we do. They're also probably in much more debt than we are, statistically speaking.

I'm laying this out not to gloat over my friends, or to say one of us is better than the other. What I'm trying to do here is illustrate that each of us has their own ideal vision of adulthood. I'm willing to forego having an apartment "on time" in the eyes of my society in exchange for less student debt and the ability to avoid taking on a car loan. My friend Missy has an apartment and a car, but also decided not to go to college. It wasn't part of her vision of an ideal adulthood, so she didn't pursue it.

The Great Recession set Millennials back in terms of hitting traditional markers of adulthood. That we can't really deny. People are living at home more and more, marriages are happening later and ages of first pregnancy are as variable as eye color. And forget about buying homes!

It goes deeper than that, though. None of us is really "on time" in terms of hitting adulthood, even if we did manage to sell an app to Google. Those of us that are managing to hit our milestones "correctly" in the eyes of Gen X-ers and Boomers are doing it through pure MacGyvering. They're inventing things, starting YouTube shows, or selling ads based on popularity of their butt selfies. So even when we win, we're doing it differently than the generations before us. We have to.

We shouldn't be sad about this. This gives us an amazing opportunity: To redefine what adulthood looks like.

In past generations, when prosperity was rampant and there was plenty of money to be made, there was a prescription to what adulthood meant. You went to college, graduated, married, bought a house, and worked until you retired. You also had a few children, and sent them to college as well.

Enter feminism, Stonewall, MTV, and the Great Recession. The rules were shattered.

People didn't want to get married if it meant they couldn't get divorced without shame. Or if they had to marry someone of the opposite sex. And what if you *don't* want children? Or if you're happy and satisfied working at a job that doesn't require a college degree?

People became more selfish, in the absolute best way you can be selfish. They realized what they really wanted, and started working for it. Marriage equality. Birth control. No-fault divorce. Labor unions. Apartments that could house families.

Now it's our turn. As one of the poorest but most social generations in history, we have the opportunity to redefine adulthood yet again. Forced to make economic compromises, we've been forced to think about what's really important.

Because let's face it: No one likes having that "adulthood update" discussion at home that makes us all feel like garbage. We're left standing with a checklist of everything we're not doing that we "should" be doing at that moment in time. We try to make excuses, saying things like, "Well, I'm working on X and Y right now. Doesn't that count?"

Of course, it doesn't count. The judgmental assholes who would judge you for not hitting all your adulthood markers on time won't ever be satisfied with what you've done. Even if you hit everything on their bullshit list, they'd complain that you didn't have enough money in your savings account while doing it. There's no pleasing people with that attitude.

What you can do is take the power back. Be proud of your choices, because that's what they are. Choices.

The truth is, of course, that we can't hit all the traditional markers of adulthood at this time. With few exceptions, the world won't let us. We have to pick and choose what we focus on. Which is freaking *great*.

It's all in how you look at things. Take Missy's situation. Yeah, she didn't go to college. She could view that as a bad thing. She had to decide between going to college or entering straight into the working world with security. She may never have a college diploma and all the respect that can come with that.

Or, she can say that the value of going straight into working without debt was the right choice for her. The appeal of a college degree wasn't strong enough to persuade her to take on incredible debt, so she chose not to go. She rejected the traditional model of adulthood, and instead chose to make a new kind. That's awesome.

Just like owning your desires, own your choices. And then use your choices to determine what kind of adulthood you want.

Instead of getting defensive during your next "adulthood update" conversation, start saying something like this: "I know I only live in an apartment right now, but I've decided that focusing on my student debt is more important right now."

Alternatively: "I know I'm not in a relationship, but I've decided that focusing on my career is more important to me right now."

"My job may be entry level, but it's more important to me to spend time with my family and save for a house right now."

"I know *you* think it's important for me to have children sooner, but for me it's more important to be secure in my relationship and finish up my college degree."

See the difference?

Let's face it: We will probably never live up to the expectations of our Boomer and Gen X-er parents. Our adulthood will never be their adulthood because the stock market crashed when we were either in college or recently graduated. The jobs weren't there. The houses were owned by adults trying to dig their way out from under a mortgage. The people we could have been dating and marrying were job-hunting as well.

We won't ever be the kind of adults that our parents expected us to be. So why even try? Just do what's important to you.

You may wonder what this has to do with minimalism. It has a lot to do with it, I promise. Because at its core, minimalism is about eliminating stuff. With redefining adulthood for yourself, you're eliminating unnecessary bullshit.

It's just like the emotional minimalism we talked about earlier in the book (you *were* talking back to me, right?). If you listen to your own desires and honor your own choices, people *do* respect you for it. You just have to give yourself the agency to do it.

Now, if you're a total rock star and manage to get all of the stereotypical markers of adulthood, that's awesome. Go you! Seriously, that's awesome. You have conquered the odds. Tweet at me, I'll throw confetti in your honor. But keep in mind just how much of an exception you are to the rule.

Also, if the idea of you not really wanting one or more of these milestones ticks you off, *good*. If you're getting angry at me right now for implying that you don't really want what you say you want, great! That's proof that you do want something but haven't figured out how to work to get it.

If this is you, feel that anger. Don't be afraid of it. Use it as fuel to work toward the future you really want. Use it as an indicator of the adulthood you want, and let it be your guide.

6

Ignore the "Experts"

My friend Tom once asked me, "What's one piece of advice you would give to college students?"

He runs a college-themed podcast, so I'll forgive him the potentially pretentious question. And I was already pretentious enough to come on as an "expert about writing." A rose on my nose.

But what did I say was the thing young collegiates should do for success? What little nugget could I pass on to Generation Z to ensure their success?

"Don't listen to everyone! Take what people say and weigh it against what *you* genuinely feel is right. Don't feel like you have to take every piece of advice from people claiming to be 'experts.'"

Throughout my entire life, I've loved hearing advice. I'm the kind of person who isn't at all shy about asking for help. I *love* it. Have any potential wisdom to pass on? Hit me!

But the people who are the quickest to dispense advice are often overconfident blowhards. These are the people billing themselves as "experts" sans credentials. And unfortunately, they're everywhere.

Which is why it's so frustrating to see people fall into traps of confusion and people pleasing after college graduation. People are offering you advice on how to live from every direction. Everyone means well, too. They're telling you to get a job here, or get a job there. Why not try an unpaid internship? How about going to grad school where your dad went? That way you can go for that medical license and live at home to save money! But don't live at home too long, that'll make you a loser and we can't have losers on our graduation record. The alumni will stop talking to us.

When you're past the post-grad phase, the advice doesn't stop coming. Now it's coming from blogs, mentors, and friends with more success than you could ever dream of. The parental advice doesn't stop coming. Ever.

Everyone means well. Genuine experts have genuine expertise.

But you don't have to listen to any of it.

Really, you don't. You *don't.* You never have to listen to anyone's advice, whatever degrees they have on their wall or followers on their Twitter account. You don't have to listen to any of that.

In fact, you are 100 percent allowed to question any expert you intrinsically feel is wrong. You don't have to say it aloud or write it in a comment. That can lead to hateful bullshit, and I don't go in for that.

What I do go in for is listening to that inner voice in your chest that says, *This sounds like fucking bullshit.*

Nine out of ten times, that voice will be right. Listening to it will make you so much happier.

The first time I heard this voice was when I was asking a relationship expert a question about my boyfriend. I was about to go abroad for two and a half months, and I wanted to know if I should abandon my relationship for the few months I was gone, or try to stay monogamous long-distance for that long.

This was a world-renowned relationship expert, and I had called in to their show. I gave this person serious cred, and still do.

But when they told me I should leave my boyfriend behind and basically have a sex-filled Eurotrip with randos, the voice inside of me said, *This sounds like fucking bullshit.*

Now, this is NOT to condemn people who took the Eurotrip option the last time they went abroad. That is a 100 percent valid choice, and I am not trying to slut-shame anyone. You people are totally fine and awesome.

In that moment, though, there was something inside me saying that that wasn't the right answer *for me.* I resented the fact that everyone (including my own mother) was telling me to ditch my relationship for months in favor of faceless guys that I may or may not run into and want to have sex with. Something didn't sit well with me with that option.

So I jet-setted to Europe, staying in my vanilla monogamous relationship. And I tell you, so much growth happened on that trip. I'm still with that boyfriend years later. And while it wasn't fun being alone romantically for that time, I learned how to be less attached to other people when it came to my own fun and fulfillment. That was something valuable I could take away from that trip, no matter how long this or any relationship lasts.

Most of all, I'm most proud of myself for listening to that inner voice. I didn't give in to something that felt unnatural to my own sensibilities.

People talk about "inner direction" all the time, but the concept is hard for a lot of folks to grasp. It's not hard to see why. Most people don't have an inner voice telling them exactly what their destiny is. It takes people some time. Hence why I advocate listening to the Bullshit Voice as much as possible. It's easier to reduce options than to add them most of the time.

That same Bullshit Voice helped me turn down jobs that ended up being too good to be true. It helped my friends decide to turn away from desk jobs that promised they would have plenty of time to work on their drawing during office hours. One colleague followed her Bullshit Voice out of a dream gig after the head management claimed that they were going to alleviate her responsibilities "next year, we promise!"

But this leads me to the more important part of this idea: You have to actually listen to any advice you hear before asking your Bullshit Voice to do its thing. You have to listen to the desk job boss, or the managers at the dream gig.

Even if something you hear is really dumb, you need to listen to it first. This is how the Bullshit Voice gets refined and informed. You have to expose it to different experts, and different sides of an issue.

You'll hear a lot of garbage. But you may also find a tiny nugget of wisdom in a sea of word vomit.

At one conference I attended, there was a lecture given by a Generic White Guy Entrepreneur. Immediately, I rolled my eyes. This guy was going to have *nothing* to teach me.

And for the most part, he didn't. On and on he droned about his generically "tragic" life story and how he overcame it to be a gazillionaire. He had one alcoholic parent who later recovered. I could find more sympathy-inducing stories on Tumblr in five minutes.

The rest of the lecture was even more tedious. A generic white guy tale of success, with a generic white guy story of success.

And then it happened. One little moment, where he said, "Family matters. More than anything. Remember that."

That tiny little nugget of knowledge sank deep into my brain. I'd heard it before, but never from someone who was actually successful. There was something so deep and resonant about it, particularly because it was coming from Generic White Guy.

You can be family-focused and still be successful. It is possible.

So even though my Bullshit Voice was drowning out most of the stuff I heard during that conference, I walked away with a tiny nugget of knowledge from that encounter.

Which is really the point of it all. Mental and emotional minimalism is really just learning how to detect bullshit, and trusting yourself to be able to detect it once it's there. It's all about trust, kids.

Well, trust and using whatever kind of cell phone you want.

7

Don't Forget About Tomorrow

You know what my least favorite piece of advice is? "Live as if every day was your last day on Earth."

I hate that advice. You know who can afford to live every day like it's their last? People who worked for twenty years in a job they hated and then retired.

If it were my last day on earth, I'd get blindingly drunk and then hop on a plane to Paris. I'd see France and then trek over to China to see everything I've always wanted to see in that country. Forget working, it's time to see the world!

If it were my last day on Earth, I'd drop acid with Lena Dunham, Woody Allen, and Tina Fey. I'd punch my enemies in the face. I'd hug and kiss my loved ones like there was no tomorrow. And in my last hour on Earth, I'd ride a motorcycle up until the last minute. And I'd keep going after I passed away! Just so it would feel like I crash-landed into the afterlife.

That'd be an awesome day. But is that really a way to live? No.

Instead, I personally prefer to spend every day making steps toward my ideal life. I write, usually a lot. I manage my social media accounts, saying hi to friends and people who like my work.

I work at my paid jobs, which I have been *freakishly lucky* to find, because they pay pretty well and aren't eating my soul. I pay bills. I buy toilet paper and orange juice.

This sounds boring because it is. But it's weirdly fulfilling to live a life that you know is part of a greater path. And honestly, that's the best you can hope for in your 20s and early 30s.

It's the best you can hope for. But that's no reason to be sad.

Let me explain with a story: In *American Beauty*, Kevin Spacey plays a guy who has one of the worst midlife crises you can imagine. He quits his high-paying job, picks up a position in fast food, and changes his life so that he has a better chance of potentially boning high schoolers. Lovely, isn't it?

Over and over again, Kevin Spacey's character reflects on his life as a freewheeling twentysomething. He mourns the immense changes that came over him and his wife once they became older and "settled." He wants that ideal life yet again, so inextricably tied to being a young person.

As Millennials, we are faced with a strange new world. We can no longer just go into the workplace and start kicking butt immediately. Or at least not all of us. We're forced to analyze our lives in a long-term way more than ever, because we don't know when our hours are going to be cut next. Or when the company we work for will go bankrupt. Or when our apartments are going to be refurbished into "luxury" models to appeal to Boomer couples, which is great for the company but makes it so twentysomethings can no longer afford to live there.

It's a freaky world. Often the temptation is to just get a job you can sit through during the day and party as much as you can at night. Live like it's your last day on earth...after you get home from your crappy job.

But that's how we end up with more *American Beauty* scenarios.

So what do we do?

We go minimalist.

I said before that minimalism is a middle ground between scarcity and hedonism. It's living at the bare minimum of stuff you need, in the interest of living sanely.

This same principle applies to life too. You can live a very fun life, but don't forget that life is also *long*. You need to plan for the future to live with balance. And balance is the true goal of minimalism.

American Beauty-esque lives aren't balanced. They idealize one specific time period of life and condemn everything that comes after it. Your twenties are for partying and not planning at all for the future. Then once you hit the age of 30-35, it's all downhill from there. You're 100 percent a grown-up. Have fun paying bills forever.

The reason lots of people become minimalists in their 30s is because that's usually when they realize that *that idea is complete bullshit.*

Why the race to accumulate so much stuff, then spend the rest of your life paying for it? Why not buy less stuff to begin with and just live as simply and happily as possible from the beginning?

We've gained very little as a society by idealizing the twentysomething stage of life. But thanks to the Great Recession, Millennials have an opportunity to define adulthood. There's a chance to begin anew, and live simply from the beginning.

I know this sounds really square. But you have to trust me: Living responsibly from your 20s on is absolutely worth it. It's worth it to de-romanticize your twenties. It sets you up to live a life that's fulfilling every step of the way.

Minimalism is all about balance, and retaining that balance in every step of life. I hope every one of you finds your own balance, and may it require even less stuff than before.

Recommended Reading

I'm not *nearly* so arrogant as to suggest you *only* read my book on minimalism to get the full story. My own philosophy is cobbled together from the works of many thinkers and writers. I suggest you look around and get many opinions on the subject. Here are the ones I found most useful!

Living with less stuff:

All My Life For Sale by John D. Freyer

This book...I can't even describe it. I found it on a library shelf when I was twelve, and it planted the seeds of minimalism into my head almost immediately. It depicts what happened when a guy decided to try selling nearly everything he owned, so that he could move to a new city with a clean slate. It ended up being an experiment on what the value of individual things can be.

The Prize Winner of Defiance, Ohio: How My Mother Raised Ten Kids on 25 Words or Less by Terry Ryan

This is an amazing book, and not just because it's a story about hustling to get by. Reading about this family's particular struggle, you get a real sense of how precious every earned item was in their lives. Appreciation (and a desire to cut back) may ensue.

Money:

Walden on Wheels: On the Open Road from Debt to Freedom by Ken Ilgunas

This is one of my absolute favorite books about money and how it can affect every bit of your sanity. Plus, learn about how one guy kicked his debt's butt and won!

Nickel and Dimed: On (Not) Getting By In America by Barbara Ehrenreich

I'm a firm believer in the idea that you can't appreciate money unless you've never had it. If you're working a low-paying job, this book will make you feel less alone and give you insight on what financial freedom really looks like. If you're at a high-paying job (lucky stuff!), you'll enjoy this gritty look at what "success" really means and how to define it for yourself.

Priorities:

He's Just Not That Into You: The No-Excuses Truth to Understanding Guys by Greg Behrendt and Liz Tuccillo

Emotional minimalism at its finest! This book's fine for both men and women, and essentially preaches that you should be no one's second choice.

Bossypants *by Tina Fey*

You are allowed to be selfish. You are allowed to call out the world on its bullshit. This book will show you the happy results that come from living this way.

Defining Adulthood For Yourself:

The Defining Decade: Why Your Twenties Matter—And How to Make the Most of Them Now *by Meg Jay*

TLDR: Life's short! Make the life you want.

Committed: A Love Story *by Elizabeth Gilbert*

"Another chick book?!" I hear you yelling. Simmer down, people. This book is recommended to all genders, because it is so lovely at breaking down a very adult-like milestone (marriage) into its bare parts. It's also basically a how-to for taking traditional "life milestones" and making them uniquely meaningful to your own life.

Wanna Hang Out and Chat about Minimalism?

O r books? Or beating debt? Or *Dark Souls*? Or anything at all?

Come find me on Twitter, at @BritMcGinnis. Yes, I meant it when I said come hang out earlier! I love hearing from folks, so definitely come by and say hello.

You can also find me on www.britmcginnis.com, or blogging in various places. Come say hello—I'm always up for hanging out!

Please Leave a Review!

Seriously, that stuff really helps me out. I want to know if and how this book helped you, what it made you think about, or what you're angry with me about. It helps me write better books and be of greater service to people looking to learn about minimalism. So please leave a brief review on Amazon!

About the Author

Just a Portland girl, livin' in a lonely wo-orld...Okay, not really. I was born in Corona, California, but later fell in love with the urban landscape of Portland. I attended the University of Oregon and developed a thriving career as a freelance writer. Pieces on traveling to Ireland and serving up relationship advice to college students have earned me many awards.

My first book, an urban fantasy titled *Gin and Brimstone* came out in summer 2014. Future works will include a speculative fiction novel, several travel-themed projects, and a six-book series centered around a women's film club. Stay tuned to my website (www.britmcginnis.com) for future writings!

www.ingramcontent.com/pod-product-compliance
Lightning Source LLC
Chambersburg PA
CBHW021145020426
42331CB00005B/913